T0167367

Seek,
Find,
Pursue

Knowing and Following
God's Calling

Jenny Deptuch

WESTBOW
PRESS®
A DIVISION OF THOMAS NELSON
& ZONDERVAN

Contents

Acknowledgments ix

Introduction...xi

Prepare for Your Calling....................................1

Think About the Tools God Has Given You.................5

Look for Needs You Can Meet....................................10

Turn Your Trials into Opportunities.........................13

Use Your Big Breaks..17

Qualify for Your Calling..20

Put Your Life into It...25

Consider Your Motives...29

Live in Obedience to God..33

Think Outside the Box...37

Be Prepared to Share Your Faith...............................40

Seek God During Uncertainty..................................45

Keep Trying..48

Get Others Involved...51

Set the Record Straight..54

Have a Good Attitude...58

Waste No Time...61

Train Up Others...64

Remove the Distractions...68

Finish What You Started..74

Ignore Your Fears...78

Don't Delay...84

Take Courage and Press On......................................88

Know When to Pursue a Different Calling....................93

Rely on God's Timing...100
Be a Fool for Christ..103
Remember the Small Stuff 107
Navigate the Roadblocks 112

Epilogue...115

Acknowledgments

First and foremost, thank You, God, for Your patience, for Your unending love, and for being my inspiration. On the days when I didn't know what to write, You gave me the words.

I'm also thankful for those in the early church who endured so many trials, persecutions, and oppositions for their faith but continued to live for Christ regardless. Their endurance, passion, and efforts set the stage for me to know about Jesus and to understand the importance of faithfully following His calling.

Thank you to my parents and brother Matt for spending countless hours editing and reviewing this manuscript. Your time, wisdom, and attention to detail were such a blessing to me, and I am certain that God will use your efforts to strengthen others in their faith.

I'm also grateful to my brothers and sisters in Christ for your support. You are my family, my home away from home, and your enthusiasm for the Lord is truly energizing.

And last but certainly not least, thank you to everyone who has been my Sunday school teacher, youth ministry leader, pastor, or mentor. This book is the result of all your planting and watering of God's Holy Word into my life.

Introduction

"Is there something more than this?" You may have asked yourself that question and pondered possible answers.

"What exactly does God have in mind for my life?" You may have thought of possibilities but found that the true answer still eludes you.

"How do I know if this is what God is calling me to?" Although you think you know the answer, you want to be sure so you don't pursue something that is a dead-end road.

What led you to this book? Are you overshadowed with the monotony of life and looking for a way to bring more meaning into it? Do you feel that spiritually you are going through the motions and want to take your relationship with Christ to a new level? Perhaps you don't know Christ at all but know that you don't like where you've been and desperately want something more for your life.

Whatever your reason may be, we have all come here for the same one. The way we've been living is no longer good enough, and we are seeking a greater sense of purpose. Indeed, all of God's creation was made with a purpose. In Isaiah 55:10–11, God tells us,

> For as the rain and the snow come
> down from heaven, and do not return
> there without watering the earth and

> making it bear and sprout, and furnishing seed to the sower and bread to the eater; So will My word be which goes forth from My mouth; It will not return to Me empty, without accomplishing what I desire, and without succeeding in the matter for which I sent it.

If God has created rain and snow with a specific purpose, how much more so has He created us with a specific purpose? God did not create anything or anyone simply because He felt like it; as verse 11 reminds us, God creates all things with an expectation that each part of creation will accomplish what He desires. Psalm 139:13–16 provides further emphasis that God has a specific purpose for us in mind.

> For You formed my inward parts; You wove me in my mother's womb. I will give thanks to You, for I am fearfully and wonderfully made; Wonderful are Your works, and my soul knows it very well. My frame was not hidden from You, when I was made in secret, and skillfully wrought in the depths of the earth; Your eyes have seen my unformed substance; and in Your book were all written the days that were ordained for me, when as yet there was not one of them.

Before each of us was even born, God took the time to plan every day of our lives—each challenge, each victory, and each activity. God planned how our lives would begin and how they would end. He gave us our personalities, our quirks, and our talents. God planned each day because He had something in mind for each of us—something bigger than ourselves and something good. He didn't send us here and equip us with certain talents or skills just to see us wander aimlessly without a purpose. Just like the rain and snow, God has sent each of us to earth because He has a purpose for us and He expects us to fulfill it.

So what is it? Are you wondering what exactly God is calling you to do? Do you want your life to be more fulfilling, to make Him happy, and to accomplish great things for His kingdom but don't know how exactly to do that? Are you unsure about how to find what your calling is? Do you want to be certain that what you think is your calling is actually what God wants?

There was another group of people who struggled with the same questions. A group of people who didn't know exactly what was expected of them, didn't know how to carry on God's purpose for their lives, and for some, didn't even realize they had a calling. This group we know as the disciples in the book of Acts.

When the book of Acts was written, Jesus had already left earth but His ministry needed to continue. Jesus was no longer around to preach the gospel, care for the sick, and help the poor. The people He left behind were now responsible for continuing what He had started. After Jesus left earth, His disciples went through a period of fear and utter confusion about what to do and how to possibly "preach the gospel to every nation," as Jesus commanded before He left. However, in the book of Acts, God revealed His purpose for each of His disciples and showed them what it truly meant to pursue the calling He assigned them and created them for.

In *Seek, Find, Pursue*, you will be journeying through the book of Acts. After reading each chapter in Acts, read the corresponding chapter in this book. In following the disciples' experiences, you too will make discoveries about what ministries God is directing you toward, how you will know what your calling is, and what will be expected of you when you find it. As you read the book of Acts, a book full of people seeking and finding God's calling for their lives, keep your own mind open to where God is calling you—and be willing to take the leap of faith to pursue it.

Prepare for Your Calling

In this first chapter of Acts, we read about Jesus' disciples seeking someone to replace Judas as the twelfth apostle. As part of the selection process, Peter laid out the requirement that whoever took Judas's place needed to be someone who followed Jesus throughout His ministry—from His baptism to His death. As we read at the end of the chapter, God chose Matthias to fill this role.

When you think about everything leading up to this event, you can see that it took a long time for Matthias to find this calling. He had been following Jesus for many years before he received this new assignment from God, but during those years, he probably wasn't bored. Having followed Jesus throughout His ministry, Matthias had likely been learning and serving in various capacities rather than just absorbing the Word and not acting upon it. As we understand more about Matthias's background and see how he responded during this selection process, there a few things we can learn about how we should prepare for our calling.

Study the Bible. We need to be prepared for when God does give us our calling. As a result, we need to be well versed and well educated in the Scriptures so that we can use them as a guide to serve in whatever ministry God has laid out for us. Studying the Scriptures may also help us see and understand what God is directing us to do.

Do good works. In the meantime, while we are waiting for God to reveal His calling to us, we should serve others and serve God. Just because we don't know exactly what our calling is doesn't mean we can't serve God in a variety of other capacities. Doing this will allow us to begin living the gospel and could open our eyes to new assignments God wants us to pursue.

Pray. Before the apostles cast lots, Matthias realized that God may have been calling him to be the apostle to replace Judas. However, before making this decision, he and the others prayed about it. Likewise, when we come to the crossroads where we think God may be directing us, we must pray and ask God if that truly is what He is wanting us to do.

Listen. We tend to think that when God shows our calling to us, He will do so with a clap of thunder or the sound of trumpets, but sometimes He will simply let us know with His still, small voice or by chance, like He did with Matthias. Regardless, when you seek God's direction, take time to listen for His response. You don't know how He will reveal your mission to you, so you must be watching and listening for when He does.

Be patient. Like Matthias, it could be years before God reveals precisely what He is wanting us to do. Seek His direction by praying, listen for His guidance, but be willing to wait for His timing.

God will reveal what His calling is for us, but we have to do our part to prepare for it. We need to seek His guidance, but we also need to do everything we can to make ourselves into the servants He wants us to be. By becoming more educated in the Scriptures and by practicing different ways of serving Him and others, we'll be better equipped to handle whatever task He assigns us. As you begin to seek your calling, seek ways to prepare for what God has planned for you.

Seek, Find, Pursue

Which parts of the Scriptures do you need to know more about?

List three ways you will make an effort to learn more about those Scriptures.

What are some ways you can serve God and others while you are waiting for your unique calling?

What potential callings do you need to pray about?

Think About the Tools God Has Given You

God will never call us to do something without giving us the necessary tools and skills to get the job done. This was certainly the case with the twelve apostles. As referenced in the Introduction, before Jesus left earth, He commanded the apostles, "Go therefore and make disciples of all the nations, baptizing them in the name of the Father and the Son and the Holy Spirit, teaching them to observe all that I commanded you" (Matthew 28:19–20).

Though the apostles surely had willing hearts, they were probably at a loss for how to accomplish this. After all, their first obstacle in spreading the gospel to every nation was the language barrier. The apostles were from Judea so they probably only knew how to speak Hebrew and Aramaic. But what about the other countries? How would they communicate with the people in Asia, Europe, and Africa? How would they master the languages of each country, much less the unique dialects of each region?

In Acts 2, we read how God meets these needs when he gives the twelve apostles the ability to speak multiple languages, but that wasn't all. The meaning of the word *language* that we find in Acts 2:8 comes from the Greek word *dialektos* or *dialects*.[1] As a result, when God gave this special gift to the twelve apostles, He not only gave them the ability to speak multiple languages, but He also gave them the ability to speak in specific dialects. As a result, when we read of the apostles using this gift, we see that when they spoke one language, the various people listening would not only hear their own language but also their own dialect.

God had called the apostles to preach the gospel to every nation, and He gave them the talents they needed to fulfill this. However, these were not the only talents we read about in the book of Acts. After Peter's sermon during the Pentecost, we read about the growing number of disciples worshipping together, studying the Scriptures, and fellowshipping together. These activities helped unite them as Christians and further spread the gospel, but it took many talents to make this happen. We read of the disciples studying the Scriptures and devoting themselves to prayer, which means there were people using their talents in teaching, preaching, and praying. We also read about the disciples sharing meals in their houses, indicating that there were people using their talents in cooking, serving, and hosting to contribute to God's kingdom. And lastly, because we read in verse 47 that "the Lord was adding to their number day by day those who were being saved," we know that there were people gifted in inviting people to church gatherings and sharing their faith.

It took many types of people to create the unity, "sense of awe," and gladness that we read about in Acts 2, and each person fulfilled their part by using the unique skills and abilities God gave them. Likewise, as we seek our calling, we should take inventory of the skills and abilities God has given us and consider how we can use them to serve Him. Some of us may be good at teaching, cooking, and serving like the people we read about in Acts. However, there are many other skills beyond that, such as encouraging, organizing, creating, and praying, all of which can be used to contribute to God's kingdom. No skill, ability, or talent is too minor to be used in God's kingdom. God gave us our abilities, quirks, and talents as tools for fulfilling our calling.

As we think about the talents and abilities God has given us, we must also realize that God doesn't give us all of them right away. Some take longer than others for us to obtain, and oftentimes, God will give us a talent without us even realizing it. The apostle Peter is a great example. In Acts 2, we read about him boldly standing up in front of a crowd of thousands and proclaiming the truth about Jesus Christ. As readers, it would be easy for us to look at Peter and think, *What a great man! He was able to speak eloquently in front of a large crowd about the Scriptures! What a brave, strong man of faith!* However, as we look back, we see that Peter wasn't always this way.

When we read about the Last Supper in Luke 22, in verse 33, Peter promises Jesus, "Lord, with You I am ready to go both to prison and to death!" Peter was ready to stand by Jesus no matter what; however, let's read further. Only a few verses later, in verse 54, we read that after Jesus was arrested, Peter followed Jesus "at a distance." Though he told Jesus he would go with Him to death, his actions proved that he wasn't brave enough to stay close by Jesus. In addition to that, in John 18 we read that Peter, when asked if he was a follower of Jesus, denied even knowing

Jesus not once, not twice, but three times. Though Peter may have thought himself to be a strong, brave man of faith, he was actually a cowardly man ashamed to call himself a follower of Jesus. However, God still had a calling for Peter, and over the course of just a few chapters in the Bible, God transformed Peter into a brave witness of Jesus Christ and an important servant in God's kingdom.

If each of us looks back, we will see that we are not who we thought we'd be and we'll see that we even have new strengths and abilities that we hadn't had before. As you seek your calling, think about the strengths, skills, and abilities God has given you, but also consider the new ones God has given to you over time. By giving them to you, God is providing the tools you'll need for your calling.

[1.] Strong, J. (1981). Language. In *The Strongest NASB Exhaustive Concordance* (pp. 629 and1520). Grand Rapids, MI: Zondervan.

Seek, Find, Pursue

What are your skills, abilities, and talents? What things are you good at and passionate about?

How can you use these to help others and serve God?

What strengths, skills, and abilities do you have today that you didn't have earlier in your life?

Look for Needs You Can Meet

It is interesting to see how Peter and John received their two callings in this chapter. In the first case, they encountered someone who had a need and asked for help. Peter and John's assignment was as simple as that. They didn't search high and low for a life-changing mission but were approached with a need. And with God's help, they met that need.

The other way Peter and John found their callings was by identifying a problem and fixing it. Society thought that Peter and John healed the lame man, but it was actually God who had done this miraculous deed *through* Peter and John. When these two men saw this misunderstanding, they worked to correct it and help society understand more about God as well.

As in Peter and John's time, our society doesn't fully understand who God is and doesn't give God the recognition, respect, and thanks that He deserves. For example, many attribute positive circumstances in life to luck rather than the hand of God. Some neglect to acknowledge God during the Thanksgiving, Christmas, and Easter holidays, and others use God's name along with foul language. Our society is in desperate need of guidance not only in respecting and honoring God but in other ways as well.

There is no shortage of needs in today's society, so once we have an understanding of the strengths, skills, and abilities God has given us, it's important for us to look for ways we can use what God has given us to meet those needs. It may be that you come across someone who needs help, as was the case with the lame man. Or you may recognize a need in society that you feel particularly called to assist with. Whatever the case may be, there are plenty of opportunities to help and to serve others, so find what suits you. Look for causes you are passionate about. Find someone in need. Or even devote yourself to random acts of kindness.

It's interesting to note that neither of the callings Peter and John found in this chapter required a long-term commitment. Sometimes, God wants us to deal with a need, situation, or a problem at hand rather than making a life-long commitment to something. Not all assignments are meant to last forever, and we are more likely to receive different callings at different times in our lives than we are to receive one that will last our whole lives. So when searching for yours, don't be reluctant to fulfill it by doing seemingly little things. Serving God and others in small ways will often help you identify a larger purpose for your life. As Jesus assures us in Luke 16:10, "He who is faithful in a very little thing is faithful also in much." So begin looking for a current need or problem that you can help with, no matter how small it may seem!

Seek, Find, Pursue

Name some people or groups of people who have asked for assistance and think of ways you can help them.

What problem(s) in society, your community, and even your church can you help change?

What is lacking in your church that you can help fulfill?

What issues do you feel need particular effort in order to turn them around?

Turn Your Trials into Opportunities

When God allows us to experience an unpleasant and scary situation, He is calling us to live for Him despite our circumstances. This was certainly the case for Peter and John who, after healing the lame man, were thrown into jail and then dragged before the Jewish Council, the same group that condemned Jesus to death. If Peter and John proclaimed the truth about God's Word as boldly as Jesus did, they could lose their lives just like Jesus. No doubt, they were probably nervous (to say the least) and discomforted about the severity of this situation.

God allows each of us to encounter similar discomforting situations. For some, it may be cancer; for others, it may be loss of a job. Even less severe situations, such as facing rejection or being ridiculed because you're different, can be equally intimidating. Whatever the case may be, these trials should not come as a surprise to us. James 1:2 says, "Consider it all joy, my brethren, when you encounter various trials." Notice that James did not say *if* you face trials; it is a matter of *when*. And trials are not limited to a certain type of challenge. James tells us that we will face "trials of many kinds"—big ones, small ones, family-related ones, work-related ones, and so forth.

When we go through these trials, it is easy to doubt God and ask ourselves, "Why is God letting this happen to me?" Though we may not completely know God's reasoning, we can get some ideas from Romans 8:28, where it says, "And we know that God causes all things to work together for good to those who love God, to those who are called according to His purpose." Though being a Christian does not guarantee us a worry-free life, being faithful to God, no matter what, guarantees that even the worst of trials will work out for good.

We see this happen with Peter and John as they stood before the Jewish Council. These men faced a very serious trial: the strong possibility that they would lose their lives because of their faith. At this point, it would have been easy for them to not put their faith first, forget about serving God, and go along to get along with the Jewish Council. But they didn't. Despite how scared they probably were, we read that they boldly and confidently proclaimed Jesus regardless of the potential consequences. The Jewish Council even ordered them to stop preaching about Jesus. However, Peter and John boldly looked them in the eye and told them in verses 19 to 20, "Whether it is right in the sight of God to give heed to you rather than to God, you be the judge; for we cannot stop speaking about what we have seen and heard."

Peter and John faced a huge trial with life or death consequences. Things were certainly not going their way, and by the looks of the situation, that would continue to be the case. However, even in the midst of this frightening situation, they still used it as an opportunity to serve God. Peter and John bravely preached the gospel in an effort to win souls and encourage others. And as Romans 8:28 promised, God used this situation for good. In verse 4, we read that 5,000 people became followers of Christ. In verse 22, we read that the people of Jerusalem "were all glorifying God for what had happened" to the lame man. And after Peter and John were released and reunited with the other disciples, we read in verse 31 that even more people began to go out and boldly spread the Word of God.

Even in this uncomfortable and scary situation, Peter and John still found a way to serve God and they were brave despite the severity of the situation. Likewise, when we are in the middle of various trials, God is calling us to be brave and to use those trials as opportunities to serve Him. Think about how you can use the trials you face to serve God, and remember that for those who love God and are called according to His purpose, the trials will work together for His good.

Seek, Find, Pursue

What kinds of trials are you facing in your life?

How can you be brave in the midst of your trials?

How is God calling you to stand boldly for Him?

How can you turn your trials into opportunities to serve God?

Use Your Big Breaks

When the apostles were in prison, they were limited to how much they could do for God. However, God gave them a big break and gave them an overabundance of a certain gift: freedom. By freeing them, God totally removed the limitations that had been placed upon the apostles. However, He didn't free them simply so they could kick back and relax; He had an expectation of what the apostles needed to do with their newfound freedom.

As we learned in chapter 2, God never asks us to do something without giving us the tools we need to do it. In this case, God knew that the apostles couldn't pursue their callings to the fullest potential if they were in prison, so He freed them so they could be completely able to do what He had wanted them to do. God had indeed given them a big break and had truly given them an unexpected surplus of freedom. But He did that so the apostles would use it to serve Him.

God gives us big breaks in many different ways. For some, a big break may come in the form of being restored to health after a long illness or being blessed with a large sum of money or another resource. For others, a period of unemployment or retirement may provide someone more time to serve God. And though many of us have not been imprisoned like the apostles were, God may have provided a big break by freeing us from situations that limited our ability to serve Him.

As we think about the big break God gave the apostles, we see in this that He gave them an overabundance of freedom. As we think about our lives and what God may be calling us to, we also need to think about what things God has given us plenty of. For some, that may be time; for others, it may be good health. It could be physical things like extra food or clothing. In the case of some of the disciples from Acts 4, they had a large amount of land. God has given each of us things (whether they are physical or immaterial) that we have plenty of, and He did that for a reason.

As God reminded the apostles, He did not give them their freedom so they could sit back and rest on their laurels. He wanted them to do something that would glorify Him. Likewise, God did not give you your big breaks or resources so you could keep it all to yourself. What will you do with what He has given you? Will you use it to serve yourself or to serve God?

Seek, Find, Pursue

What big breaks has God given you in your life?

What are some things that God has given you in abundance?

How can you use the big breaks and the abundance of resources God has given you to serve Him?

Qualify for Your Calling

The seven men who were chosen to help the widows received their callings rather quickly. There was a need that required immediate assistance and the apostles delegated it to these seven men. These seven may not have been actively searching for a calling, but their callings certainly found them!

However, what is important to note about this chapter is that as we search for our mission, we need to work on preparing ourselves for whatever God may be directing us toward. The qualifications set forth for the seven men in this chapter also serve as great requirements for us to meet so we can be well prepared to pursue the task God gives us.

As Acts 6:3 lays out, the first requirement we must meet is to be "of good reputation." A strong reputation is important for us as Christians, because it will give us credibility when we pursue our callings. Let's go to 1 Timothy 3. This chapter describes the character traits one should have if he wishes to be an overseer at the church. Among many other traits, this chapter specifies in verses 4 to 5, "He must be one who manages his own household well, keeping his children under control with all dignity (but if a man does not know how to manage his own household, how will he take care of the church of God?)" This is a very poignant question and adequately points out that if one cannot control one's own household, one will not be credible enough to manage God's house.

Though many of us may not be seeking the role of an overseer in the church, these same rules apply regardless of whatever assignment God may give us. By taking that question we read in 1 Timothy, we can apply that same logic to our own lives and our own callings. "But if a man does not know how to manage his finances, how can he encourage others to pursue financial stability?" "But if a woman cannot stay away from sexual immorality, how will she be able to teach others to stay away from it?" "But if parents cannot take care of their own children, how can they take care of the orphans in Africa?" The list could go on and on, and you can fill in the blanks with your own examples as well. However, the overall message is that if we are not living the way God has commanded us to, we cannot encourage others to do the same. When people hear us teaching to live a certain way but see us doing the opposite, they will think we aren't a credible source of advice. As a result, they won't grow closer to Christ and will probably stay farther away from Him. In order to be effective in pursuing our callings, we must ensure that we have a godly reputation both within our church and outside of it.

Another qualification we need to consider is the presence of God's Spirit. When specifying what was required of the seven men needed to serve the widows, the apostles stated that they needed to be "full of the Spirit and wisdom." This also applies to us regardless of what task God gives us. Let us think about the "full of the Spirit" part of this requirement. If God's Spirit does not live in us like it should, how can we show others the way to find it? If we are not guided by God's Spirit, how can we guide others with it? And most importantly, if we do not have God's Spirit with us, how can we find our callings in the first place? The presence of God's Spirit allows us to directly communicate with Him and helps us make sure that our thoughts and actions are in line with what Christ wants. Without His Spirit, our efforts on God's behalf would be empty and fruitless.

If you do not have God's Spirit in you and want to make His Spirit a part of the everyday workings of your life, you must be baptized. In Acts 2:38, Peter encouraged others, "Repent, and each of you be baptized in the name of Jesus Christ for the forgiveness of your sins; and you will receive the gift of the Holy Spirit." As indicated in this verse, we receive God's gift of the Holy Spirit after we are baptized, so baptism is essential for us to have access to God's Spirit. Upon your baptism, you will not only have the presence of God's Spirit as you seek your calling, but you will also be better prepared to pursue whatever tasks He calls you to do.

Lastly, as Acts 6 points out, it is also important for us to be full of wisdom. As we have learned so far and as we will continue to learn as we go through Acts, God calls us to serve Him by living a godly lifestyle in addition to doing good works. In order for us to do both, we must have knowledge and wisdom of what God commands in the Bible. After all, if we don't know what God expects of us, how can we live accordingly or encourage others to do the same? By attending church, going to Bible studies, and reading the Bible on our own, we can increase our spiritual knowledge and wisdom and be better able to pursue our mission. Though it may seem that some have more biblical knowledge than we do, we shouldn't be discouraged. One can never have enough knowledge or wisdom regardless of how much he or she may already know. Having a thorough knowledge of the Scriptures is something we must constantly pursue, and the more we know, the better equipped we will be when it's time to pursue our callings.

As you consider your calling and where God may be directing you, think about how well you meet the qualifications set forth in Acts 6. Make every effort to have a good reputation to those around you. Take the steps to make God's Spirit present in all aspects of your life. And lastly, spend time in the Scriptures so you will have the wisdom you'll need for the tasks God assigns you. The more qualified you make yourself, the better God will be able to use you for His purposes.

Seek, Find, Pursue

What aspects of your life are damaging your reputation as a Christian?

How will you get your heart right with God and establish a better reputation for yourself?

What steps will you take to make God's Spirit a greater presence in your life?

How will you make an effort to increase your wisdom and knowledge of the Bible?

Put Your Life into It

Many would look at Stephen and say that he had an extreme calling because it cost him his life, but what Stephen gave is no more than what we are required to give. Anyone who chooses to follow God and serve Him must be willing to give up their lives for Him. In Matthew 16:24–25, Jesus tells us, "If anyone wishes to come after Me, he must deny himself, and take up his cross and follow Me. For whoever wishes to save his life will lose it; but whoever loses his life for My sake will find it." However, the command to give up one's life for Christ not only applies in an absolute sense but also in a symbolic one.

Giving up our lives to God doesn't only mean physically dying should the need arise but also that we must let go of what we want out of life and must put God's wants above everything else. It means dying to self and living only for God and His purposes. How do we do this? We must first understand what dying to self truly means. In John 14:15, Jesus said, "If you love Me, you will keep My commandments." If we are truly to die to self and live for Christ, we must follow His commandments and obey Him in all things. Because Jesus was perfect and we are but humans, we need to realize that we have sinned against Him many times, disobeyed Him, and disappointed Him. Despite all that, we read in 2 Peter 3:9 that God does not want any of us to perish but desires that we repent of our sins.

Once we have realized our need for God's forgiveness, we need to do what Peter preached in Acts 2:38. "Repent, and each of you be baptized in the name of Jesus Christ for the forgiveness of your sins; and you will receive the gift of the Holy Spirit." Not only must we repent of our sins, but we must also be baptized. Romans 6:4–7 tells us that when we are baptized and immersed in the water, it symbolizes the death of our old self that was once living in sin. When we come up out of the water, it symbolizes the birth of a new person, someone who no longer wants to be involved in sin and is committing to obey Jesus' commands. When we are baptized, we no longer seek to please ourselves but seek to please God.

As a result, as Christians, we are not only called to believe in God but we are also called to live like we believe in Him. After repenting of our sins and being baptized, we must continue to live our beliefs by doing what 1 Peter 3:11 says. "He must turn away from evil and do good; He must seek peace and pursue it." It is not enough for us to repent of our sins and be baptized. We must continually seek to do what is right in God's eyes and avoid sin at all costs. By doing this, we not only can look forward to spending eternity with Him, but we will also set an example for others to follow.

God doesn't call everyone to physically lose their earthly lives on His behalf like Stephen did. But He does call everyone to lose their self and sin-centered lives and instead fully live for Him all the days of our lives. God does not settle for gaining half of our lives. He wants all of it, and with God, it is all or nothing. If you have not joined the many who have given up their lives for God and His purposes, do not wait. Giving up your sinful life for Him will not only help you draw closer to Him but will also make you more effective in fulfilling the calling He has for you.

Seek, Find, Pursue

What are some things you need God's forgiveness for?

What steps will you take to ensure that you keep Christ in the center of your life and stay away from sin?

Consider Your Motives

It is important that when we do *anything* to serve God, we do it for the right reasons, and we can look to Simon the magician as an example. Simon thought his calling was to give the Holy Spirit to people, but Simon wasn't seeking to serve God in this. Simon was looking to entertain people and perhaps even make some money out of it. As a result, his motivations were very displeasing to God.

Why are you searching for your calling? Are you looking to show off or draw attention to yourself? Are you doing it to impress someone or to win the approval of people? Are you trying to gain earthly benefits, like money or power, by serving God? If you answered yes to any of these questions, you are one of the many Christians who have made this mistake. Many of the "greats" in the Bible, like Moses and even Jesus' own apostles, made the mistake of serving God in order to bring attention to themselves or because they wanted something out of it.

However, this attitude is not pleasing to God and *must* change before we look for our callings. Philippians 2:3–4 tells us, "Do nothing from selfishness or empty conceit, but with humility of mind regard one another as more important than yourselves; do not merely look out for your own personal interests, but also for the interests of others." Once we have made the decision to serve God, we must remember that our wants and interests no longer matter; it is God's desires that need to be most important in our lives. Thankfully, God gives second chances to anyone who has put himself first and wants to make God first instead.

How do you change your attitude from wanting to please yourself rather than God? Let's look at what Peter advised Simon to do. Simon was told to repent of his wrong intentions and to seek God's forgiveness for his sin. Likewise, whenever our intentions aren't God-centered, repentance and seeking forgiveness are always the first steps to change. We must wholeheartedly apologize for what we have done wrong, ask for God's forgiveness, and then try not to repeat the same mistake again.

Many times, repenting and seeking forgiveness is the easiest part of this process, and it is often more difficult to prevent making the same mistakes again. Though it is hard to break a bad habit or wrong intentions, God will help us change if we ask, and He has given us the Scriptures to help us. For example, Philippians 2:3–4 can be used not only to help us examine our own intentions but also to evaluate whether God is truly directing us to pursue a certain path. As you think about what your calling may be, ask yourself some questions. Does this calling stem from *selfishness and empty conceit* or *humility of mind*? Would this calling serve *your personal interests* or *the interests of others*?

Simon was so caught up in his personal interests that he convinced himself that God was calling him to give the Holy Spirit to others; however, this was not at all the case. Simon's selfishness made him think that God was asking him to do something that God didn't want him to do at all. In fact, Simon's attitude and behavior were displeasing to God. As you search for your mission, stop to examine yourself to make sure your motives are focused on glorifying God and not yourself. If they are focused on self-glorification, you can be sure that your potential calling is not in line with what God really wants. Work to change your heart so that it can truly be used to serve Him. God is waiting with open arms to help you change, and with His help, you can change your heart and accomplish great things for His kingdom.

Seek, Find, Pursue

What selfish ambitions do you need God's forgiveness for?

As you pursue your calling, what will you do to take the focus off yourself and move the focus to God?

Live in Obedience to God

For Saul, there were two stages he went through to find his calling. The first was to change from his sinful ways and instead choose to serve God. God can use *anyone* to accomplish things for His kingdom, but in order for Him to do that, we must first prepare ourselves by ceasing to live a life of sin and instead living a life dedicated to God. In Saul's case, he was caught up in the sin of persecuting Christians, and God literally stopped him dead in his tracks of sinfulness to show him that what he was doing was wrong. Only after that was God able to use Saul to serve in His kingdom.

The second stage that Saul went through was to spend time in Damascus. It is interesting to note that Saul *did not* find his calling on the road to Damascus; he received it sometime after he reached Damascus. In verse 6, Jesus told Saul, "Get up and enter the city, and it will be told you what you must do." It was only after Saul obeyed what Jesus commanded that he found his mission. Many think that when they receive their callings from God, they will find them during a dream, a vision, or perhaps even a blinding light, but this isn't so. It is only as we live as God commands that we will find them.

So once he reached Damascus, when exactly did Saul find his calling? The Bible isn't specific, but by examining Saul's time in Damascus, we can make some educated guesses as to what he did while he waited. Once he reached

Damascus, the Bible says that, for three days, Saul didn't eat or drink. So with no food, no drink, and no eyesight, Saul probably did a lot of thinking and praying. The Bible also says that Saul was baptized and then spent some time with the disciples in Damascus afterward. During this time, Ananias told Saul that God was calling him to be a witness to others about what God had done in his life (Acts 22:12–16). However, exactly when Saul found his calling isn't important. What is important is how he prepared himself to find it.

He prayed. God will reveal His calling to us, but we must first ask. By praying, we acknowledge that God is in control and that He will show us what He is wanting us to do. One of God's favorite ways to communicate with His people is through that still, small voice, so it is not only important to pray and seek guidance but also to listen with an open mind and a willing heart.

He got baptized. Saul's baptism not only symbolized his desire to serve Christ but also demonstrated his absolute obedience to God's commands. When searching for our mission, it is important for us to follow all God's commands (including baptism) so that our hearts will be ready to receive what God has planned for us.

He spent time with fellow Christians. When you are with other Christians, you can encourage each other and hold each other accountable to live in obedience to God. By serving together, your brothers and sisters in Christ can also give you insights as to what your gifts are and how you can use them to serve Him. Finally, when you do receive your calling, your brothers and sisters in

Christ will give you the help and moral support you need to complete the tasks that God has assigned to you.

Obedience is essential for us to find our callings. It is only after we rid our lives of sin and practice living according to God's commands that we can expect Him to reveal His purpose for us. If Saul hadn't been obedient to God, he couldn't have encouraged others to do so. And if he hadn't submitted to God by obeying His commands, he couldn't have possibly submitted to God by fulfilling his ministry. God will use us to serve in His kingdom, but we must prove to Him that we are willing to do whatever He tells us, big or small. Seek to live in obedience to God, and once you have done this, you'll find that your calling won't be too far behind!

Seek, Find, Pursue

What sins are keeping you from fully serving God?

What steps will you take to get these sins out of your life?

List three ways you will make an effort to live obediently to God.

Think Outside the Box

Ultimately, God wanted Peter to preach to Cornelius and his family, but before God directed him to do that, He prepared him. Peter testified in verse 28 that it was against the Jewish law to associate with people who were not Jewish (or "Gentile"), so under the constraints of that law, evangelizing to Gentiles like Cornelius was not an option. As a result, Peter and the other apostles were only witnessing to the Jews. But in this chapter, God showed Peter a new way of looking at His kingdom.

Another law under the Jewish culture at that time was that Jews were forbidden to eat animals that were considered unclean, such as pigs, rabbits, and eagles. As a result, you can imagine Peter's shock when God lowered down a sheet full of clean *and* unclean animals and told him he could kill and eat any of them. However, when God told Peter "What God has cleansed, no longer consider unholy," He was introducing Peter to a new way of thinking. And this new way of thinking would not only impact Peter's eating habits but would more importantly change the way he served God. Because in this chapter, God showed Peter that everyone—Jewish or not—needed to hear the Word of God.

This was a totally different concept for Peter to grasp, and it was probably hard to no longer believe something he was raised to believe. However, in order for Peter to complete the assignment that God had for him, he needed to first think outside the box and be ready to do something new and different. And this is exactly what Peter did. Immediately afterward, Peter paid a visit to Cornelius and his family, people who would formerly have been considered unworthy of hearing God's Word. Peter enthusiastically preached the gospel to them, baptized them, and saved their souls as a result.

Many Christians who are pursuing their callings will tell you that they never dreamed they would be serving God in those particular capacities. You'll even find ministers who would never have imagined receiving a call from God to serve Him in that capacity. However, the beauty of God's plan for our lives can be seen in Isaiah 55:8, where God tells us, "For My thoughts are not your thoughts, Nor are your ways My ways." There may be aspects of our lives that make us feel inadequate to serve God, and there may be some types of assignments we would quickly dismiss as not being the right ones for us. But God doesn't think like we do, and despite what we may think, God can still use each of us to do new things for His kingdom. Because He will ask us to do new and unimaginable things, we must prepare ourselves by having open hearts and open minds.

Serving God and pursuing His calling for your life means taking leaps of faith. Reflect on the questions below and know that your potential callings are not impossible. As Mark 10:27 says, "All things are possible with God," so don't let doubt keep you from pursuing your calling!

Seek, Find, Pursue

How is God calling you to do something "outside the box" for His kingdom?

What are some things you have thought of doing but thought were impossible for you?

What are some things you have thought of doing but are too afraid to try?

Be Prepared to Share Your Faith

As you live your life as a Christian, there will be times when people question why you choose to follow Him and why you live the way you do. Though this may seem intimidating, this is very often a calling from God to witness to others about Him. This happened to be the case for Peter. The apostles in Judea not only questioned Peter but also criticized him for introducing the saving power of Jesus Christ to the Gentiles. (The other apostles were still living by the former way of thinking, which was that Jews could not associate with Gentiles). Nevertheless, it was probably daunting to not only be criticized for his service to God but also to be criticized by his fellow Christians.

No matter what ministry you pursue, you will encounter criticism from Christians and non-Christians alike. People will question why you are living the way you are, people will criticize you, and some will think you are crazy. But when this happens, it is important that you handle those situations just like Peter did—by serving God anyway and responding to opposition in an orderly and patient way. Though the other apostles were wrong for criticizing Peter, they truly didn't understand why Peter had done what he did. Peter realized that their criticism came from a lack of understanding, and instead of retreating or lashing out at them, Peter took the time to teach them.

Many of us have experienced times when others have

questioned our relationship with Christ or have criticized us because of it. And for many of us, if we had been in Peter's shoes looking at a large group of people who were demanding an answer, we would be getting weak in the knees. However, when God calls you to do something, He doesn't necessarily call you to do something that requires a lot of training or practice. Sometimes, it is just a matter of using a past experience to glorify Him. In response to their questioning and criticism, Peter did not prepare a sermon, he didn't debate them, and he didn't spend a few months in seminary preparing his response. Rather, he just recounted to them an experience and how it led him closer to God.

Simply telling people how God has worked in our lives can be used to accomplish great things for His kingdom, and that was certainly the case in this chapter. After Peter related his experience to his fellow Christians, they glorified God, were reenergized in their faith, followed Peter's example and went themselves to preach to the Gentiles, and saved many souls as a result.

Through this adversity, God was calling Peter to be a stronger witness to others. However, telling others about how God has impacted your life is not just a good idea; it is essential. Later on in the New Testament, we find some critical words that speak to how we must witness to others, even in the face of adversity.

> But even if you should suffer for righteousness' sake, you will be blessed. Have no fear of them, nor be troubled,

but in your hearts regard Christ the Lord as holy, always being prepared to make a defense to anyone who asks you for a reason for the hope that is in you; yet do it with gentleness and respect, having a good conscience, so that, when you are slandered, those who revile your good behavior in Christ may be put to shame. For it is better to suffer for doing good, if that should be God's will, than for doing evil.

Do you find encouragement from those verses we just read? Do they bring you hope? Do you know who wrote them? Peter. The verses we just read were penned by the same Peter who was questioned and criticized for his faith but stood and defended his faith anyway. The verses we just read were written by the same man who learned firsthand just how essential it is for Christians to be prepared to stand up for their faith. And who knows whether it was his experience in Acts 11 that inspired him to write these encouraging words in 1 Peter 3:14–16?

People will criticize you and question you for your faith. As a result, we as Christians must always be prepared to give a reason for why we live the way we do, why we chose to follow Christ, and why we put our hope in a God that is unseen. We must not be afraid when these times come but instead must confidently defend our faith and know that God will bless us for standing up for Him.

When the time comes for you to share your faith,

don't be afraid, because God will never call you to do something that is beyond your capability. Instead, during those times, confidently use your past experiences to show others the way to God. And no matter how intimidating the situation, know that God will bless you for it.

Seek, Find, Pursue

Recount some times when people have asked you about your faith or criticized you for it.

When people ask you about your faith, what stories will you share with them that will show them how God has worked in your life?

Seek God During Uncertainty

When we finally have found our callings and start to pursue them, we will come to a point when we wonder whether God is wanting us to do that anymore. Since most tasks are not meant to last a lifetime and may only last for a time, how will we know when God no longer wants us to pursue our assignment?

Peter faced the same predicament when he was put in prison. Jesus had commanded Peter to preach the gospel to all nations, and Peter had only just begun this when he was suddenly put in prison for doing what Jesus had commanded him. Peter probably had his doubts about his ministry while he sat in prison, and he must have been wondering if God was no longer wanting him to be a preacher. After all, one of his fellow disciples, James, had just been killed for preaching the name of Jesus, and Peter had been arrested with the same purpose in mind. As for Peter, by worldly standards, it was impossible for him to break out of prison. He sat between two guards, was chained not once but twice, had more guards outside the door, and had an iron gate keeping the prison securely locked.

Peter's ability to continue with his calling looked pretty bleak at this point. However, though Peter may have doubted the possibility of being able to continue, God found a way to make it happen. God overcame all the things that made it seem like Peter would no longer pursue his mission, and God gave Peter the opportunity to serve Him again. Indeed, Jesus' words "With man this is impossible, but with God all things are possible" (Matthew 19:26 ESV) were still proving to be true even in Peter's seemingly hopeless situation.

God is the one who gives each of us a calling, and it is only God who can tell us when it is complete. At those times when we begin to wonder whether God still wants us to pursue our callings, we must not doubt or give up too quickly. Instead, we must spend time reading His Word, praying and seeking guidance, and asking our brothers and sisters in Christ for their prayers as well. If we seek His wisdom, God will direct us where we need to go whether it be continuing with our callings or pursuing different ones. But most importantly, we must remember that when things seem impossible, God can still overcome and we need to trust Him to pull us through the seemingly impossible.

Seek, Find, Pursue

How will you seek God's guidance when your calling looks more and more impossible?

Name some brothers and sisters in Christ who can guide you when your calling becomes uncertain.

Keep Trying

How will people respond to us when we pursue our callings? In all honesty, we will probably get the same kinds of responses that Paul and Barnabas did—a mixture of positive and negative.

When Paul and Barnabas arrived in Antioch, they received a very positive response. Not only did the leaders of the synagogue invite them to preach, but they were also invited to come and teach the next week! And what is more, that next week the whole city came to hear them preach! The people were desperate to hear the Word of God, and many became Christians due to Paul's and Barnabas's efforts. However, though there were many who were anxious to hear the good news, there were also many who didn't want it preached at all. These people persecuted Paul and Barnabas so much that they eventually pushed them out of the city.

When we pursue God's calling for us, we will not always elicit a favorable response for our efforts. Though some will be receptive to the message we bring, some will be marginally receptive and others will be downright opposed to our efforts and may even try to stop us. However, we should not let this discourage us from pursuing our mission. Not everyone that Jesus ministered to became followers, and even Jesus had people who were utterly opposed to His ministry and tried to stop it from succeeding. In fact, when Jesus sent his twelve apostles out to preach the gospel in Matthew 10, we read Jesus telling them in verse 14, "Whoever does not receive you, nor heed your words, as you go out of that house or that city, shake the dust off your feet."

Jesus didn't say *if* they weren't received; it was a matter of *when*. Jesus knew from experience that not everyone would be receptive to the Word, and He wanted to prepare his apostles for this. Jesus went through the worst possible opposition by suffering a horrible death on the cross. Why should we expect any more success or any better treatment than Jesus had?

And though they had received a negative response from some of the people in Antioch, Paul and Barnabas did something that was very important. When they were pushed away, they didn't lament the lack of enthusiasm for their ministry; rather, they shook the dust off their sandals and kept trying. Paul and Barnabas knew that their efforts would be more effective if they looked for people who would be interested in the message rather than wasting their efforts on those who weren't. Indeed, they took Jesus' advice from Matthew 7:6 (NIV). "Do not give dogs what is sacred; do not throw your pearls to pigs." By following this guidance, Paul and Barnabas were able to reach out to a much larger group of people who were truly overjoyed to hear God's Word.

So when you don't get a good response to your efforts, do not be discouraged. Instead, keep trying and focus your efforts where they will have the most impact for God.

Seek, Find, Pursue

What parts of your calling should you stop pursuing so you can make a more impactful difference elsewhere?

What are some areas of your calling where you can refocus your efforts?

Get Others Involved

When pursuing your calling, it is important to get other people involved. This can be beneficial in a number of ways, but first and foremost, it is important to include others because you will be able to support and encourage each other. God didn't want Adam to be alone, so He created Eve. When Jesus sent out His apostles to spread the good news in Matthew 10, He sent them out two by two. Indeed, Jesus felt not only that two hands are better than one; He also thought that each person can serve to help and encourage each other.

This was certainly the case for Paul after he was stoned. Acts 14:19–20 says, "They stoned Paul and dragged him out of the city, supposing him to be dead. But while the disciples stood around him, he got up and entered the city." If Paul didn't have that support group to help him, he probably would have died and his ministry would have ended too soon. But, as we read in Ecclesiastes 4:9–10, "Two are better than one because they have a good return for their labor. For if either of them falls, the one will lift up his companion." This was certainly the case for Paul and should be the same for us. When we pursue our ministry, it is also important to have a support group so that we don't get too discouraged and so we have someone who can help us up during the hard times.

However, having help as you follow your mission is important in another way; it gives others an opportunity to serve God. In Hebrews 10:24, we read, "Let us consider how to stimulate one another to love and good deeds." Part of our role as a Christian is to "stimulate" others to do good deeds and to commit acts of love. While this can be done by encouraging others in their walk with the Lord, it can also be done by asking for help with your calling. Think about it. Think back to a time when someone asked you for help. How did you feel? Weren't you excited that someone had sought you out and asked for your assistance? Didn't it make you feel valued? Weren't you anxious to help that person?

That's exactly how it would be if you asked others to help you with your ministry. Let's think back to chapter 3 of this book. You were asked to think about individuals or groups of people who asked you for help, because there was a possibility that you could find your calling simply by helping those people. But you know what? It works both ways. If you need help fulfilling God's purpose for your life and you ask others for help, you are stimulating others to do good deeds and helping them find their purpose too. And what better way to carry out your calling than by helping others find theirs?

As you ponder what God's ministry is for you, think about who you can ask to help you and how they can help. Whether it is through prayer, supplying resources, or serving along with you, getting others involved gives you a support group in times of challenges and stimulates others to be enthusiastic servants in God's kingdom.

Seek, Find, Pursue

What are some areas that you need help with as you pursue your calling?

Who can you ask to help you in these areas?

Set the Record Straight

In this chapter, there was a disagreement between two cultures over whether one had to be circumcised to be saved. As the apostles preached the gospel, they found themselves caught between the beliefs of two cultures: the Jews, who believed circumcision was essential for salvation, and the Gentiles, who didn't believe circumcision was necessary and who didn't want to follow the traditions of the Jews. The newly converted Christians who were teaching these things had grown up with the law of circumcision in the Jewish religion, and because circumcision had always been required for salvation, they continued to teach this. However, this was no longer correct and was even causing the Gentiles who were thinking about converting to Christianity to see Christianity as overly burdensome.

As a result, God called Paul and Barnabas to set the record straight and to show their fellow Christians, and ultimately the Gentiles, the lifestyle God desired from believers. They did this in two key ways.

They let the Holy Spirit lead them. In verse 28 of this chapter, Paul, Barnabas, and some other apostles explained, "For it seemed good to the Holy Spirit and to us to lay upon you no greater burden than these essentials." God had given the apostles the Holy Spirit to help them discern right from wrong, and rather than simply going with whatever teaching sounded good at the time, they meditated, prayed, and used the Holy Spirit to guide them as they confronted this difficult issue. As a result, they were able to discern and to teach others the correct way.

They used the Scriptures to find the answers. A disciple named James quoted Scripture that described how God would rebuild the requirements for His followers and how God would make a relationship with Him available to all people. As a result, the church leaders determined that some of the commands the Jews had abided by previously would no longer be critical for Christians moving forward. James didn't teach this based on his personal opinions; he used the Scriptures to find the truth.

The people in this situation were unclear about the correct way to live, and they had been teaching that certain actions were essential in God's eyes when in fact they weren't necessarily required at all. Unfortunately, the same problem exists today. Many religious denominations teach that abstaining from meat on certain days or praying to saints is important for salvation. Society will also teach that certain lifestyles, like promiscuity and immorality, are acceptable in God's eyes, but this couldn't be farther from the truth. And like Paul, Barnabas, and the others, we are called to set the record straight and to lovingly show others the right way to live.

God doesn't necessarily call us to change the world or to accomplish some grandiose task. A lot of times, He simply wants us to set the record straight and to show people the right way to live. There are many ways we can do this. For Paul, Barnabas, and the other apostles, it was by preaching, writing letters, and encouraging others to live God's way. For us today, it may be showing others what the Bible truly teaches about certain issues, giving our time or resources to a Godly cause, or teaching Christian principles in our own families. Whatever the case may be, God wants each of us to set the record straight so that others will come to know more about Him.

Seek, Find, Pursue

What issues do you need to address in order to set the record straight?

How will you help set the record straight?

Have a Good Attitude

We often think of a calling in terms of actions, but what about our attitude? We can do all the right things, but if we don't do them with an attitude that pleases God, it is all for nothing.

Let's look at Paul and Silas. After preaching the gospel, encouraging the churches, and standing for Christ, they were beaten with rods and attacked by a crowd. They were then thrown in prison and put in shackles. At this point, they could have been angry at God, could have lamented ever choosing to follow Him, and could have complained that He let them down. But instead, they fulfilled an even greater purpose by maintaining a positive attitude. Though they were beaten, worn, and uncomfortable, even in the midst of prison, Paul and Silas prayed and sang songs of praise to God so that all could hear.

And they did hear. In fact, in verse 25, we read that "the prisoners were listening to them." The prisoners may not have known who God was, but they were listening. They may have been bitter about their current situation, but they were paying attention to Paul's and Silas's living testimony.

It is interesting to read on and see that when the doors of the prison were opened, none of the other prisoners left. Why do you think this is? The Bible doesn't say for sure, but perhaps Paul's and Silas's joyful and peaceful attitude during trials made the other prisoners want to see how they could find that peace and joy for themselves. Perhaps they felt that if they followed the guys who were happy even in the midst of challenging situations, they could find happiness and peace too.

We need to be the same way. Our actions and attitudes should glorify God so much that people will look at us and say, "I want whatever that person has in his or her life." Even in the midst of our worst nightmares, God is calling us to live for Him and shine His light. And very often, it is in the midst of our worst nightmares that our lights shine the brightest. As you walk through dark times in your life, will you reject God or will you use the dark times to be a shining light for Jesus?

Seek, Find, Pursue

What trials are you going through that require you to keep a positive attitude toward God?

How is God calling you to use your attitude to glorify Him?

Waste No Time

In this chapter, there's one thing you must admire about Paul. He wasted no time. In verse 16, we are told that he was waiting for Silas and Timothy to arrive so they could continue preaching on their missionary journey. Paul could have used this waiting period to get some sleep, take some time and relax, or even do some sightseeing in Athens. However, Paul instead chose to use his waiting period to serve God.

While he was waiting, he looked around and saw a need for people to know Jesus, and rather than kick back and enjoy his time off, he did something about it and witnessed to the Athenians. We read in verse 17, "So he was reasoning in the synagogue with the Jews and God-fearing Gentiles, and in the market place every day with those who happened to be present." Paul not only witnessed to those who knew God and worshipped him but also witnessed to people who didn't know God at all. Even in the market place, Paul would spread the good news about Jesus to anyone who was there. Paul didn't stop and take a break; we read that he did this every day.

And Paul's persistence paid off. Before he knew it, he was discussing Scriptures with the leading philosophers of the time and was then requested to go before the Areopagus, the Athenian court, to share the ministry of Jesus with the public leaders. And on Mars Hill, the place where the Athenians would go to gaze upon the temples of their gods, the Athenians were instead learning about the one true God and the ministry of His Son Jesus Christ. Paul made an important impact on the Athenian society and expanded the reach of God's kingdom simply because he refused to sit around and do nothing.

Paul had been in a waiting period in this point of his life, and it would have been easy for him to stand back and be silent while he was waiting for the time to pass. However, God was still calling Paul to use that time to serve Him and further His kingdom. In Colossians 4:5, Paul testifies to the value of time and advises each of us, "Conduct yourselves with wisdom toward outsiders, making the most of the opportunity." Paul knew from personal experience that even the waiting periods of life offered opportunities to reach out and share the good news of Jesus, and God used Paul's efforts to have an incredible impact on a society that didn't know Him.

Are you in the middle of a waiting period in your life right now? Are you waiting to find a new job, waiting in line at the market place like Paul, waiting to hear results from the doctors, or the like? No matter what you are waiting for or how long you are waiting, God is calling you to use your waiting periods to serve Him and reach out to the lost. Sometimes, all it takes is a word of encouragement or a prayer to effectively use your waiting period for Him, so don't waste time. Think of how you can serve God during the waiting periods of your life!

Seek, Find, Pursue

What waiting periods are you going through right now?

What waiting periods do you face on a daily basis?

How will you use your waiting periods to serve God?

Train Up Others

Sometimes, it's easy to see the ministry of Apollos and to think that each of us has to have a ministry of that magnitude as well. However, behind the success, reach, and effectiveness of Apollos's ministry were the true unsung heroes in this story: Priscilla and Aquila.

This couple served God and spread His Word by ministering to people in their own community: Apollos in this chapter. After listening to Apollos preach, Priscilla and Aquila kindly set the record straight in the areas where his preaching wasn't quite correct. From there, Apollos took what he learned from Priscilla and Aquila and in turn traveled to many countries and preached the gospel to those who needed to hear it.

Priscilla and Aquila's contribution may appear small, but it certainly wasn't. Think about what would have happened if they didn't teach him the correct way and just let Apollos continue along with his ministry. Apollos would have reached many people with his ministry, but he would have been teaching them things that weren't completely correct. And as we read in Matthew 15:14 (NKJV), the Bible cautions about incorrect teachers and says that "if the blind leads the blind, both will fall into a ditch." Though Apollos would have had good intentions, by teaching things that weren't completely correct, people wouldn't have had the right understanding about God that they should have had.

However, Priscilla and Aquila chose to take time to teach Apollos and train him better for the task God had set before him. And what was seemingly a small contribution paid off in dividends. We read in verse 27 and 28, "When he had arrived, he greatly helped those who had believed through grace, for he powerfully refuted the Jews in public, demonstrating by the Scriptures that Jesus was the Christ." Apollos had a huge impact on society, but the reason he was able to do this was because someone took the time to teach him.

Some Christians are called to begin what we'd call a "high impact" ministry that reaches to other cities and countries. However, it is equally if not more important for others to stay and serve on the home front. And just as God has directed some people to be missionaries outside the hometown, He has also chosen many to stay and train up the next generation of God's servants.

Perhaps you've had hopes of leading a "high impact" ministry and it hasn't reached the level you had wished for. Or perhaps you are discouraged when you compare yourself to the "high impact" servants in God's kingdom and think that because your ministry is not at that level, you're not making a meaningful difference. Don't be discouraged! Perhaps God is not asking you to be the front man but is calling you to stay and minister to those at home. If all Christians were front men, who would train up the next generation of front men?

There's absolutely no shame in being the behind-the-scenes person that prepares others for a greater ministry. Apollos certainly had a powerful ministry as he traveled to foreign countries to preach the gospel, but he had that because somebody had taken the time and effort to teach him, mentor him, support him, and prepare him for his ministry. By correcting Apollos's teaching, Priscilla and Aquila not only impacted Apollos but also the people Apollos taught later. As you ponder God's calling for you, contemplate how God can use you to train up others for their callings. You may end up being like Priscilla and Aquila and become the person to ignite and fuel a powerful ministry for God's kingdom.

Seek, Find, Pursue

How can you support those who are getting ready to start a new ministry?

How will you help train up others for their callings?

Remove the Distractions

Many incredible things took place in this chapter, and the good news of Christ spread in mighty ways. However, the most incredible feat for God's kingdom came in how the people of Ephesus changed their lives to follow Jesus.

As we read about Paul's efforts in Ephesus, we read about many exorcists and people who practiced magic. At the time, Ephesus was the center for witchcraft and many cult-like activities. Consequently, many people (like the exorcists and silversmiths we read about) made their living off these practices. For the people of Ephesus, black magic, cults, and serving other gods was a way of life; children grew up learning these practices and the citizens actively participated in them. These ungodly activities were so prevalent in society that they became how Ephesus defined itself.

However, when we read of Paul's ministry in Ephesus, we learn that many of the Ephesians not only believed but also completely changed their lives as a result. In verses 18 and 19, we read,

> Many also of those who had believed kept coming, confessing and disclosing their practices. And many of those who practiced magic brought their books together and began burning them in the sight of everyone; and they counted

up the price of them and found it fifty
thousand pieces of silver.

This was a huge step in the lives of the Ephesians.
For them, black magic and cults were a major part of
everyday life. Those activities were deeply engrained in
the traditions, beliefs, and the values of that society, and
to the Ephesians, there was no other way of life. For
the people in Ephesus to confess their practices and to
essentially proclaim that everything they knew to be true
about life was wrong was an incredible feat.

However, the Ephesians even went a step further and
took all of their books about witchcraft and burned them.
This speaks volumes about the faith of the Ephesians and
the extent to which they felt God calling them. It would
have been really easy for them when they heard Paul's
preaching to casually confess to their ungodly practices
but hang on to their books. But the Ephesians, though
they didn't know much about God, knew enough to
realize that God didn't just want them to confess that
what they were doing was wrong; He also wanted them
to totally eliminate those practices from their lives.

God gave a similar calling to the Israelites from
Mount Sinai when He gave the Ten Commandments.
The number one commandment He gave was this: "You
shall have no other gods before Me." Period. It is easy for
us to think of the word "gods" and to think that that word
just means a statue or object that someone worships, but
that is not the case at all. A god is *anything* that distracts
you from your relationship with Christ and causes you to

take your eyes off Him. For some, that may be money. For others, it may be fame. For the Ephesians, it was black magic. God knew that if the Ephesians had kept those books in their houses, they would have been tempted to forget about Him and revert back to the old, sinful way of life. As a result, God called the Ephesians to completely rid themselves of the things that would cause them to sin, and the Ephesians, though very young in their faith, recognized that calling and were faithful to it.

However, the Ephesians' willingness to burn their books also spoke volumes to the community around them. Ephesus was the center for witchcraft, yet these Ephesians felt so strongly about their faith and they were so certain about the truth of God's Word that they "brought their books together and began burning them in the sight of everyone" (vs. 19). The Ephesians' change of life was not a secret; those who continued to practice witchcraft watched as these new Christians publicly professed that they would stop living according to the sinful ways of their society. What a testimony! Imagine what a statement it was to see people not only rejecting the sinful activities of society but also destroying anything that would connect them to that society! What a testimony to their faith and their belief in Jesus Christ!

However, the depth of the Ephesians' living testimony can also be found in examining the value of what they gave up. They burned so many books that the value of everything they burned amounted to a value of 50,000 pieces of silver. That already sounds like a lot, but let's take it take it a step further and put this value in perspective.

Back then, one piece of silver was worth a day's wages. That means that the value of everything that was burned amounted to 50,000 days' worth of wages, or 137 years' worth of wages. Stop and think about that. A total of 137 *years'* worth of wages was burned and completely destroyed.

We don't know how many people participated in this book burning, but we can safely assume that in doing this, many were giving up their livelihood. Many were destroying their life's savings. Everything they worked for in life was gone and their means for providing for themselves was gone. But to these Ephesians, none of that mattered, because they knew that their relationship with God was far more valuable than their career, their standing in society, and 137 years' worth of hard work.

In Matthew 16:25–26, Jesus says, "For whoever wishes to save his life will lose it; but whoever loses his life for My sake will find it. For what will it profit a man if he gains the whole world and forfeits his soul?" The Ephesians realized that it was far better to rid themselves of the things they valued most than to forfeit their soul, and they immediately responded to this command from God. What about you? What things in your life are distracting you from God and keeping you from fully pursuing His calling for you? Perhaps it's pornography; perhaps it's money. Perhaps books or movies in your home cause your faith to deteriorate. Or maybe it is witchcraft, as it was for the Ephesians.

Whatever the case may be, God wants each of us to rid ourselves of the things that will harm our relationship with Him. He is calling us to completely destroy and eliminate anything that will cause us to stumble in our faith or distract us from fully serving Him. If we don't do this, what does that say about our love for Christ? If we don't do this, what does that tell others about our faith?

The Ephesians were mere infants in their faith. They didn't know a lot about God and they didn't know every commandment in the Scriptures, but their faith was so strong that they were willing to burn everything that would distract them from Christ. I pray that you, whatever stage of your relationship with Christ may be, will be willing to do the same and give up what you value most for the sake of Jesus.

Seek, Find, Pursue

What addictions, distractions, and gods in your life stand between you and your relationship with Christ?

How will those things hinder you from pursuing your calling?

How will you eliminate these things from your life so you won't forfeit your eternal soul or your calling?

Finish What You Started

Are you pursuing your calling and feeling discouraged? In taking up this ministry, are you coming across challenges or obstacles that make it look like it's impossible to fulfill? Perhaps you feel like you have lost your inspiration to continue, or perhaps the work involved no longer seems worth it.

If you feel discouraged or have been thinking of giving up, don't let it stop you because among those feelings is another calling for us—a calling to finish. In the course of Paul's ministry, he faced many challenges. He was beaten, put in jail, and rejected by those who didn't want to hear what he had to say. And if that wasn't enough, Paul admitted in this chapter that the future didn't look that bright either.

However, in verse 24 (ESV), Paul states, "But I do not account my life of any value nor as precious to myself, if only I may finish my course and the ministry that I received from the Lord Jesus, to testify to the gospel of the grace of God." Paul knew what his mission was, and though there were many challenges ahead, he knew that he still wasn't finished fulfilling it. Paul knew that there would be times when he would experience discouragement, pain, and heartache in his life as a result of his calling. However, Paul realized that the thing that was more valuable than his life was to finish the calling God had laid out for him. Paul knew it was more important to minister to those with him and to "help the weak" than it was to avoid the challenges and discomfort his ministry would bring him. And despite the challenging and uncertain future ahead, Paul pressed onward, giving God and his ministry everything he had.

But unlike the Ephesians, God gave us the privilege to see Paul on the other side when he finally finished. And we read Paul testify in 2 Timothy 4:6–8,

> For I am already being poured out as a drink offering, and the time of my departure has come. I have fought the good fight, I have finished the course, I have kept the faith; in the future there is laid up for me the crown of righteousness, which the Lord, the righteous Judge, will award to me on that day; and not only to me, but also to all who have loved His appearing.

As we read Paul commenting on his life, it becomes clear why he didn't consider his life of any value—he knew what was ahead for those who finished. Paul was able to look back on his life, see all the challenges he went through, remember all the times he was tempted to doubt that God was with him, and to recount standing for what was right even when no one else would. But after looking back on the challenges, pain, and discouragement he went through, Paul, now standing at the finish line, was able to look ahead. Paul was able to look forward to an eternal life with Jesus Christ, and he was able to leave this life in peace and with no regrets.

And his advice to those he left behind? In verse 5 of that same chapter, Paul tells us, "But you, be sober in all things, endure hardship, do the work of an evangelist, fulfill your ministry." When pursuing our callings, we *will* face challenges, we *will* face discouragement, and we *will* entertain thoughts of giving up. But just as God called us to start with our callings, He is also calling us to finish what we started. This life will be hard, but there is a great reward to those who cling to Christ during the tough times and serve Him wholeheartedly during the challenges. God has brought you this far, and He promises to bring you the rest of the way. So don't give up on your calling now, because the best is yet to come!

Seek, Find, Pursue

How have you been tempted to give up on God's calling for you?

What steps will you take to endure the challenges and completely fulfill your calling as Paul did?

Ignore Your Fears

This chapter brings about a critical point in Paul's pursuit of his calling. God had made it clear that He wanted Paul to preach the gospel in Jerusalem, and now Paul had to make a decision. He could either obey God or let fear prevent him from being all that God called him to be.

Indeed, Paul was surrounded by fellow Christians who knew that preaching in Jerusalem would lead him to be bound and delivered into the hands of the Gentiles, and as friends and brothers, they were concerned for his safety and well-being. But Paul, convicted and convinced of the importance of his ministry, declared, "For I am ready not only to be bound, but even to die at Jerusalem for the name of the Lord Jesus" (v. 13). Paul knew there would be serious consequences for preaching in Jerusalem, and he knew that this assignment would come at his own personal expense. However, Paul also knew that he existed to please God, and as such, he chose to ignore his fears and relentlessly pursue God's calling despite the cost.

Many of us will face a similar choice when given our callings. However, oftentimes, we will see what God assigned us and instead of pursuing it passionately like Paul did, we let fear prevent us from following through. Some of us may have fear because we know we'll face persecution as a result. And some of us may simply fear this new ministry because it would change our plans and conflict with what we want and desire. However, it is these moments that define our faith and test our commitment to following God's lead. God certainly does not take these moments lightly, so when we face these times, it is important that we are like Paul and have the courage to be obedient to God's calling despite our fears. To do this, there are a few things that we need to keep in mind.

Let's start by looking at 2 Timothy 1:7 (ESV). In this verse, Paul himself writes, "For God gave us a spirit not of fear but of power and love and self-control." God is the giver of power, love, and self-control, but one thing He does *not* give us is a spirit of fear. That is simply not something God passes on to those who follow Him. So if it's not God who gives us a spirit of fear, than who is it? Satan. As God's Enemy, Satan will do everything in his power to prevent God's plan from being successful, and as a result, when God shows you your calling, Satan will do everything he can to discourage you from pursuing it. Many times, the tool he uses to accomplish this is a spirit of fear—fear of the unknown, fear of leaving your comfort zone, and fear of being inadequate. When these thoughts enter your mind, remember that they are from Satan and not from God. In fact, when those thoughts discourage you from following your calling, it's probably even further proof that that's the calling God wants you to pursue.

Because God doesn't give us a spirit of fear, that also means He didn't create us to be people who shrink away from our callings. God's purpose for us is to be people who courageously follow our mission regardless of the potential consequences. The author of Hebrews speaks to this in chapter 10 when he describes followers of Christ who endured tough trials and encourages others to do the same.

> But remember the former days, when, after being enlightened, you endured a great conflict of sufferings, partly by being made a public spectacle through reproaches and tribulations, and partly by becoming sharers with those who were so treated. For you showed sympathy to the prisoners and accepted joyfully the seizure of your property, knowing that you have for yourselves a better possession and a lasting one. Therefore, do not throw away your confidence, which has a great reward. For you have need of endurance, so that when you have done the will of God, you may receive what was promised. *For yet in a very little while, He who is coming will come, and will not delay. But My righteous one shall live by faith; And if he shrinks back, My soul has no pleasure in him.* But we are not of those who shrink back to destruction, but of those who have faith to the preserving of the soul.
>
> —Hebrews 10:32–39

The author of Hebrews explains that enduring life's challenges will help guarantee that we are worthy of eternity with Christ when He returns. The author encourages the Hebrews (and us) to maintain our confidence in Jesus Christ during those times so that we will receive what God has promised to His faithful. As we read from those verses, we are not a people who shrink back during the tough times; God has made us for much more, and He will reward us for overcoming our fears and enduring the challenges, including those we may face as we fulfill our ministry.

A final thing to keep in mind is that neglecting to follow God's direction brings dire consequences. James 4:17 tells us, "Therefore, to one who knows the right thing to do and does not do it, to him it is sin." Pursuing our callings is not just about doing the right thing; it is also about preventing ourselves from sinning against God. Oftentimes, we pray and ask God to show us our callings and somehow think that when God shows them to us, we'll have the option to tell Him, "No thanks. That's not something I'd be interested in after all." Other times, we may see pursuit of our ministries as way to earn "extra credit" for our faith, not as something that's required from God. However, James makes it clear that is not the case. Neglecting to do the right thing is sin, and as we read earlier in Hebrews, God takes no pleasure in someone who shrinks back from obedience.

Many of us in pursuit of our callings will come to a crossroads just as Paul did, and we will have to decide whether to keep going or whether to turn and run away.

During those times, it is likely that Satan will give us a spirit of fear to scare us away from being obedient to God's purpose, and during those times, we will be forced to make a critical decision. We can choose to sin against God and shrink away or we can be the people He created us to be: a people who courageously obey Him regardless of the potential consequences. Paul chose to ignore his fears and pursue his calling anyway. What will you do?

Seek, Find, Pursue

What are some things that cause you to fear pursuit of your calling?

List three ways you can overcome those fears.

Name three people you can rely on to encourage you and strengthen you when you get fearful about continuing with your calling.

Don't Delay

Though we've only read a little about Paul's conversion experience on the road to Damascus, in this chapter, Paul describes some more of the details of his conversion and how he received his calling to be an apostle. As soon as Paul received his sight, God communicated to him (through Ananias) what He wanted Paul to do. And as soon as Ananias explained to Paul what God expected of him, he asked Paul a very pertinent question: "Why do you delay?"

God didn't waste any time after Paul received his sight to give him his calling, and in return, He didn't want Paul to waste time getting started. The same thing goes for us. When we decided to become Christians, God ran to us with open arms and rushed to bring us the joy and blessings that come with following Him. He also immediately called us to live our lives differently and to work to further His kingdom. We all know what we have to do, but we all find excuses for why we "haven't gotten around to" pursuing God's purpose for our lives. Though we're all guilty of this, we must strive to pursue our callings with as much urgency that God had in giving them to us. And just like Ananias asked Paul, God asks each of us, "Why do you delay?"

In Luke 12:42–47, Jesus compares the blessings of following God's calling to the consequences of not following it.

And the Lord said, "Who then is the faithful and sensible steward, whom his master will put in charge of his servants, to give them their rations at the proper time? Blessed is that slave whom his master finds so doing when he comes. Truly I say to you that he will put him in charge of all his possessions. But if that slave says in his heart, 'My master will be a long time in coming,' and begins to beat the slaves, both men and women, and to eat and drink and get drunk; the master of that slave will come on a day when he does not expect him and at an hour he does not know, and will cut him in pieces, and assign him a place with the unbelievers. And that slave who knew his master's will and did not get ready or act in accord with his will, will receive many lashes."

God has many blessings in store for those who faithfully and urgently pursue their purpose, but He also has dire consequences in store for those who delay and put it off. As the verses above point out, Jesus is coming back at a time we do not expect. What if He comes tomorrow and finds us having not begun to fulfill His calling for us? What will we tell God when He asks us why we haven't started? It will be too late to make the excuses that God won't accept. As a result, we can't afford to delay any longer. We must start now before it is too late!

Seek, Find, Pursue

Do you delay? What reasons do you have for not pursuing your calling as urgently as God would have you to?

How will you overcome this?

Take Courage and Press On

Up to this point, we have mostly discussed ministries that are related to things we enjoy doing or take pleasure in accomplishing. However, not every calling we receive will be an enjoyable one or one that we look forward to. In fact, many will put us through trials, pain, and suffering.

Paul faced this same challenge as the soldiers brought him to speak to the high priest. So far, Paul's testimony about Jesus' resurrection had not been well received by the Jews in Jerusalem. Because his testimony and teachings about Jesus were so different from their teachings, the Jews felt he had committed a religious crime that warranted a trial before the high priest. In the course of this, Paul recognized that the high priest was disobeying the law by punishing prisoners without a fair trial. At this point, Paul had a choice to keep quiet about the issue or to point out that what the high priest was doing was wrong. Though the latter option certainly would not endear him with the religious leaders, Paul chose to speak out against what was wrong. How's that for being an unpleasant calling?

And if that wasn't unpleasant enough, Paul boldly took this calling a step further and addressed a disagreement among the people in the council about Jesus' resurrection. Because the Sadducees didn't believe in Jesus' resurrection and the Pharisees did, they were not unified in how they worshipped God or in how they judged prisoners like Paul. Once again, Paul could have chosen to ignore this issue and let it pass, but he chose to bring the problem out into the light so that people would recognize it and fix it. As with most problems, Paul's situation worsened before it improved. When Paul addressed this issue, the Pharisees and Sadducees argued with each other to a point where Paul had to be taken away in order to protect his life.

Paul had truly upset the hornets' nest by addressing these two unpleasant matters, but he still chose to do the right thing regardless. And because of this, God brought him through the challenges at hand. In verse 11 of this chapter, after Paul spoke up against these two issues and was put back into Roman custody, we read something that is very comforting. "But on the night immediately following, the Lord stood at his side and said, 'Take courage; for as you have solemnly witnessed to My cause at Jerusalem, so you must witness at Rome also.'" While Paul was in a very frightening and uncertain place in his life, God communicated three important things to him.

1. **God was at his side.** Even in the depths of prison and even in the midst of total opposition, God was at Paul's side and would continue to be as long as Paul continued to obey God's calling.
2. **Take courage.** One of the most frequent messages God sends Christians in the Bible is "Have no fear." How many times do we hear God telling his followers to have no fear or to be courageous? The Bible is full of these reminders, and in this chapter, God reminds Paul to take courage through his challenges. Why? Because God was at his side.

3. **God wasn't done with him yet.** We've read of numerous challenges Paul faced as he followed God's purpose for him, and having been beaten and thrown in prison again, Paul may have been wondering if his ministry was over. But God reminded him that He still had plans for Paul to continue. Rather than Paul's imprisonment being a sign that his calling was finished, it was actually a sign that God had more in store for him.

As He did with Paul, God will sometimes call us to do things that are completely unpleasant and undesirable. Perhaps it is to show a person or a group of people that what they are doing is wrong. Perhaps it is to preach a message that someone doesn't want to hear. When we are given an assignment that will potentially bring us grief or aggravation, we will be tempted not to do it. We may even think that it is too much for us to handle.

But God thinks differently. God wouldn't give us a calling if He didn't think we could handle it, and if He gives you one that seems to be too challenging, He is doing it because He has you in mind for the job. Not your neighbor and not your coworker. He wants *you* to do it. If God has confidence in you, how can you not have confidence in yourself that you can follow through with a difficult assignment?

Just as God stood by Paul's side and told him to take courage and keep trying, He does the same for you. And just as God brought Paul safely through the difficulties he had, He will do the same for you. So take God's hand and take a leap of faith, because with Him by your side, you can tackle the most challenging calling.

Seek, Find, Pursue

What are some challenging callings God has placed in your life?

How will you take courage in the face of those challenges?

Know When to Pursue
a Different Calling

As we read about Paul regularly speaking before Felix and then being sent back to prison, it's interesting to consider whether that calling to witness to Felix got tiresome after a while. Sure, Paul probably put his absolute best into it, but there may have been times when he got discouraged and possibly even wondered if there was another ministry out there beyond the one at hand.

Likewise, as each of us pursues God's calling, there will be times when we face the same question. There will be times when it seems monotonous, repetitive, or simply just doesn't make us as excited as it used to. It is these times when we will consider whether God wants us to keep pursuing that ministry or maybe move on to another one. As you pray and seek to know what's next, there are a few things you should keep in mind.

First of all, ask yourself if the ministry in which you serve still needs you. This is not a trick question, and don't take this question personally. God always needs servants in His kingdom; however, sometimes a ministry will grow to a point where it has become self-sufficient and doesn't need as much hands-on assistance as it used to. When it reaches that point, it may be time for you to consider a new assignment. Think about Paul and his ministry. As we've seen in the book of Acts, when Paul first started a church, he would stay with that church for a certain period of time (usually a year or so). During that time, he would teach the people and train up leaders to serve the congregation. After those leaders were comfortable with the Scriptures and with leading the church, Paul would leave and start another church somewhere else.

Paul would recognize that the people he trained now had a handle on the ministry, and because of that, he wasn't as needed to preach sermons, lead Bible studies, or mentor people. As a result, rather than having two people do the work of one, he would see his assignment as being finished and would then move on to the next one. When we reach situations like this and we are not as needed for a certain ministry as we used to be, we shouldn't take this personally; in fact, we should joyfully celebrate this! Any time a ministry grows and expands, that is something we should be truly thankful for. However, when these situations happen, it could also be that God's assignment for us is complete and it's time to work on a different one.

Another thing to think about is whether God is still giving you the resources to continue in your current ministry. We learned in chapter 2 that God will never give us a task without giving us the tools to get that task done. Think about your current ministry. Is God still giving you the tools you need for that task, or are you lacking them? Perhaps you no longer have the passion for your ministry that you used to. Maybe that ministry demands more money or other resources that you can no longer provide. Or perhaps you are physically not able to do a lot of the things you used to, making it difficult for you to continue with a calling that demands physical abilities. Just as God will give us what we need to do a task, He also will not expect us to continue with the task if we don't have what we need. So if you no longer have the resources needed to continue with your ministry, then maybe it's time to ask God what's next.

On the flip side, if you're thinking about doing something new, has God given you the resources to pursue that? In Paul's case, he was confined to prison, so he couldn't just get up and leave for another missionary journey. He couldn't head downtown to feed the homeless or even to teach at the temple. Paul did not have the resources (aka the freedom) to leave and pursue a new calling. As a result, Paul continued with his current mission—to witness to Felix and those in prison.

What about you? Is there anything that is preventing you from pursuing a different ministry? For example, if you're married and have children, it would be very difficult to leave for a yearlong overseas mission trip. If you are of modest means, it will be difficult for you to be the next great philanthropist. And all of those things are okay. Each of us has limitations, but it's important to determine which of those would prevent you from pursuing a new calling. And if they do prevent you, maybe God is telling you to stay where you are.

Do you feel challenged in your faith? Though our callings should almost always be focused on benefitting others and God, it is also important that they benefit us personally—specifically, in challenging and building our relationship with Christ. Pursuing a new calling often requires us to leave our comfort zone. It challenges our faith, because it forces us to abandon what we know we can do and instead to depend on God, communicate with Him, and seek His direction in ways we haven't before. However, once we have reached a point where we have mastered that ministry, feel like we are going through the motions, and don't feel challenged in our faith, then it's time to pursue a new one. We can't let our relationship with God become stale and monotonous, because that gives Satan an opportunity to distract us from Him. Our faith should always have some form of discomfort, because that forces us to seek God and to rely on Him more.

With that in mind, think about whether the ministry in which you serve is still challenging your faith. Do you feel like you've outgrown it? Are you relying on God more or less than you used to? Do you feel challenged in your faith, or do you feel like you're well within your comfort zone? If you think that your current calling is not building your relationship with God like it used to, it is probably time to seek a new one that will challenge your faith and take your relationship with God to the next level.

Finally, if you've been thinking about all these things and still are not sure whether or not to seek a new ministry, there's one more thing to keep in mind: no excuses! As we read in chapter 1, while we are searching for God's calling, we should be finding ways to serve Him in the short term, just as Matthias likely did during Jesus' ministry. A lot of times, serving God by doing "short-term" projects will open our eyes to new opportunities. It will also bring us closer to others who can guide us as we seek a bigger mission. So even though you're unsure exactly what your next opportunity will be, don't let it be an excuse to not serve Him. Get involved with your church, serve others, and keep seeking God's wisdom. When the time is right, God *will* let you know where to go next.

Seek, Find, Pursue

Does the ministry you're serving in still need you, or has it become self-sufficient?

Is God still giving you the tools needed to pursue your current calling? Are you lacking the tools, and if so, what are you lacking?

Has God given you the resources to pursue a new ministry? If so, what resources has He given you to do this?

Is your current ministry challenging your faith? Are you as close to God as you were when you started with this ministry or do you feel like it has become stale and monotonous?

List five ways you can serve God while you're determining where to go next.

Rely on God's Timing

On the surface, it may seem easy to begin something that God has called you to do. It also might seem understood that as soon as God directs us to do something, we would begin right away. However, though that may be the case sometimes, there will also be times when God asks us to do something but doesn't give us the opportunity to start until much later.

Let's take Paul as an example. In chapter 23, after testifying before the Jewish Council in Jerusalem, God told Paul that he would have to testify in Rome as well. Two chapters later, in Acts 25, Paul appealed to Caesar so that he could indeed go to fulfill this calling. However, as we read in Acts 24:27, Paul was in prison at least two years before he got to this point. It wasn't until two years after God first gave Paul this assignment that Paul was actually able to start pursuing it.

As Paul sat in prison for those two years, there may have been times when he was frustrated that he didn't have the opportunity to begin what God had tasked him to do, and he may have even wondered if God had really wanted him to testify in Rome in the first place. We may experience the same thing in our own lives. We may feel like God has called us to do something but, for whatever reason, the timing is not right or there isn't the opportunity for us to begin. However, as we've seen with Paul's experience, sometimes God will give us a task that we need to begin immediately, but sometimes, He will plant seeds in our hearts that may not come to fruition until much later. Just because Paul didn't go to Rome right away didn't mean that God wasn't calling him to witness there; it just meant that Paul had to go to Rome at the right time in order for his testimony to be most effective. The same goes for us. If we're not able to begin our ministry immediately, that doesn't mean God doesn't want us to do that task; it may just be that God wants us to wait for the right time.

Should we sit back and relax while we wait for the opportunity to present itself? Absolutely not! Even Paul, during his two-year stay in prison, frequently came before Felix and preached Jesus until he had the opportunity to appeal to Caesar and go to Rome. He didn't sit around and wait for the opportunity to find him; he made every effort to seek out the opportunity. The same should be said for us. Though God may not plan for us to begin our callings until much later, there is no reason why we shouldn't actively be seeking the opportunity to begin them. Indeed, Hebrews 11:6 confirms that God rewards those who diligently seek Him.

As you think about the various ways that God is calling you and as you think of the various stages you may be in fulfilling them, don't be discouraged if some of them haven't gotten off the ground yet or if you find yourself still waiting for the opportunity to present itself. Diligently seek God, and with His help, you will find the chance to begin your calling at just the right time.

Seek, Find, Pursue

In what ways has God called you but hasn't given you the opportunity to begin them?

What callings have you given up on that you should try to begin again?

Be a Fool for Christ

Paul boldly gave his testimony to Festus and King Agrippa, and he confidently put his all into this opportunity that God had presented to him. However, as he was wholeheartedly preaching the gospel to this audience, the first response he received was "Paul, you are out of your mind!" In the eyes of God and the eyes of Paul, what he was doing made perfect sense, but in the eyes of the world, he was out of his mind. The world couldn't understand why Paul was living the way he was living. The world couldn't understand why he clung unwaveringly to his belief that Jesus died, rose from the dead, would return one day to judge, and wished for all to come to Him. They couldn't comprehend why Paul was so passionate about making people disciples of Jesus. To them, it was nonsense.

But in this lies incredible encouragement for us as Christians. We often look at Paul and see him as one of "the greats" in the Bible. We admire his commitment to Christ, his perseverance in the face of trials, and the many ways he served God. However, even a "great" like Paul was thought by some to be out of his mind. And if such a negative comment could be said about someone so strong in the faith, what should stop the world from saying that about us?

Nothing. And in all actuality, we should expect to receive comments similar to what Paul received. In

Matthew 5:11, Jesus said, "Blessed are you when people insult you and persecute you, and falsely say all kinds of evil against you because of Me." In this verse, Jesus did not say *if* people insult you; it was a matter of *when*. Jesus made it clear that living for Him would elicit ridicule from others, so if someone isn't being ridiculed on Jesus' account, then what could that say about their faith? It may be that it's not a true faith. Because true faith means being different. True faith means being "weird" by the world's standards, and the Bible is full of examples of just how "weird" we should be.

First Peter 2:9 (KJV) says that we are "a peculiar people." Verse 11 in that same chapter says we are "aliens and strangers." In 1 Corinthians 4:10, Paul tells us, "We are fools for Christ's sake." Peculiar? Aliens? Fools? Verses like that make someone like Paul look like he fit in perfectly. By totally devoting his life to his calling, Paul earned the title of someone who was out of his mind, but he was doing exactly what God wanted him to do. God doesn't want us to be like everyone else. He wants us to stand out and be different. He wants us to live our lives in such a way that people think we're peculiar, and if we do anything less, we must consider whether we are living up to our full potential for God.

That could sound discouraging, but it is actually a source of great encouragement. In Matthew 5:12, after telling us that we will be insulted and persecuted for our faith, Jesus then tells us, "Rejoice and be glad, for your reward in heaven is great; for in the same way they persecuted the prophets who were before you." If we are being ridiculed and teased for our faith, we are in good company and we are joining the many who have gone before us and lived their lives as fools for Christ. However, as we endure the ridicule of the world, it is also encouraging to know what awaits us on the other side.

As you consider the ways God is directing you, also think about the fervor with which you pursue your calling and your relationship with Christ. God will reward those whose fervor earns them the reputation of being foolish, strange, or out of their mind. Will you be one of those? With the reward you know is ahead, you'd be foolish not to!

Seek, Find, Pursue

How have you been ridiculed, made fun of, or teased for your faith?

What steps will you take to ensure that you remain foolish in the eyes of the world and worthy in the eyes of God?

Remember the Small Stuff

This chapter started off as a simple sailing from one city to another. Paul (and many of those with him) had been on sailings before, and this one seemed to be no different. However, what started as a routine sailing quickly turned into a worst nightmare for those involved. For two weeks, their ship was driven and tossed by a severe storm, bringing intense fear and agony to those onboard. They tried everything they could to alleviate the storm's impact on the ship—they adjusted the sails, threw away the extra cargo, and even tied ropes around the ship to hold it together. But their best efforts were no match for the hurricane-like storm. Having lost control over the ship, failed all attempts to escape, and seeing no end in sight, all hope of being saved was abandoned.

Could you imagine being in this situation? Could you imagine being in a completely chaotic and uncontrollable situation, seeing no light at the end of the tunnel, and having absolutely no hope? That's the situation these people were in; they could only wish to see light again, and they had nothing solid to cling to. Except for one person: Paul.

Even in the midst of this completely hopeless situation, Paul had faith and Paul indeed had something solid to cling to. What did he do? He shared it with those who had none. When others had given up hope of being saved, Paul shared God's promise that they would be safe. When others were completely drained from fighting the storm, Paul fed them. And when seeing daylight only seemed like a distant wish, Paul gave thanks to God for what they did have. And what happened? They were encouraged! Paul's actions not only gave them an emotional boost but also gave them the energy to fight the storm another day. Though his words of encouragement may have seemed like an insignificant offering, they truly meant the world to those who received it. And for those who received it, it was the difference between having something to live for and having no hope at all.

When we think of the calling God has for us, our minds oftentimes shift to big things—being a missionary to a foreign country, planting churches, or starting the next big revival in our community or nation. But more often than not, the seemingly small things can make just as great an impact. Let's take Paul as an example. During the storm, if Paul had decided to give money to his shipmates, the money would have done them no good. If Paul built them a new, shiny ship, it would have been useless. What those around him needed and what they truly craved was encouragement.

Encouragement is underrated in today's society. Many times, we think that giving money or accomplishing some incredible act of charity is the solution for every problem, but it's not. Oftentimes, it is the small things like a personal touch and word of encouragement that are truly the solution during the storms in life. And just as God called Paul to encourage those around him, He calls each of us to reach out in "small" ways and encourage others who may have lost hope.

When you look around, you'll see that there are people all over who have totally lost hope. Perhaps some have lost hope in saving their marriage, maybe others have lost hope in being able to feed their families, and perhaps some are just overwhelmed with the storms of life and have lost the will to go on. These people are everywhere, and it is the job of each of us to reach out to them and encourage them. Perhaps it's by sharing the hope we have in Christ. Perhaps it's by giving them a hug or a shoulder to cry on. Maybe it's giving them an "Atta-boy!" or "You can do it!" when things seem uncertain. Or it could even be praying for them or feeding them like Paul did. Whatever the case may be, your "small" acts of kindness and words of encouragement can be the one thing that turns someone's life around, and it could literally be the difference between life and death—both physically and eternally.

As you go through life, realize that your calling is not always to something extraordinary; oftentimes, it is something seemingly small and ordinary that God uses to have an eternal impact on others. In 1 Thessalonians 5:14, Paul gives advice as to how we should conduct our lives as Christians, and among the things he advises, he tells us to "encourage the fainthearted, help the weak." If encouragement and helping others weren't important, Paul wouldn't have mentioned it, but Paul knew that the seemingly small stuff was often the sole solution when all other efforts failed. Will you deliver that solution to those who are desperate for it? You never know whose storm you will turn around.

Seek, Find, Pursue

Who are some people you know of that have completely lost hope?

What are some "small" steps you will take to give them the hope they need?

Navigate the Roadblocks

We just finished reading about a man who received many callings and who followed through with them fully and wholeheartedly. This man was beaten, thrown in jail, and persecuted for following God's purposes, but despite that, he was still able to fulfill all of them.

In this chapter alone, we see numerous examples. Paul had been shipwrecked and bitten by a snake on the island of Malta, but he still managed to heal the sick while he was in that place. As he continued his tiresome and seemingly endless travel to Rome, he still went out of his way to visit with his brothers and sisters in Christ wherever their ships went to port. At the end of the chapter, we read that Paul was under house arrest for two years, but he still preached Jesus to all who visited him. What we read in this chapter was only a taste of the trials and challenges that Paul went through, but despite all of that, Paul still figured out a way to pursue his calling.

Now it is time to look at the story of your calling. God has called you to do many things and to serve in many capacities to ultimately bring Him glory. You will face challenges and you will face persecution, but just as He did for Paul, God will ensure that you will never be totally hindered from pursuing your mission. Though you may become limited in some ways, you can still overcome the roadblocks, fulfill God's purpose for you, and bring His light to those who don't have it.

God will never ask you to do something without giving you the tools to get it done, so be assured that you will never be completely prevented from serving Him. So as you go out and pursue God's callings for your life, do so knowing that He will help you navigate the roadblocks that come.

Seek, Find, Pursue

What things could hinder you from pursuing God's callings for you?

How will you overcome those roadblocks in order to finish the tasks God has set before you?

Epilogue

We started this book with a number of questions: How will I know when I've found my calling? What does God want me to do? How do I fulfill God's calling for my life? And as we've journeyed through the book of Acts, we've discovered new things about God, His purpose for each of us, and His expectations for you personally.

We've discovered that God doesn't always communicate His calling through a clap of thunder or even through a life-changing experience; oftentimes, He uses a simple request for help, a chance situation, or a broken society to reveal His desire for you. Regardless of how He chooses to communicate it, we as Christians must be willing to listen. And as the book of James points out, we must "be doers of the word, and not hearers only" (James 1:22 ESV). Listening to God and knowing your calling isn't good enough; we must be willing to get out and do it!

We also discovered that God's calling for each of us may be more than we think. We found that God calls us to do many things, not just one thing at a time. We learned that God will ask us to do unpleasant things, not just things we enjoy. And lastly, very often God will direct us to do something seemingly impossible, something that appears way beyond what *we* define as "doable." Regardless of how many ministries God is calling you to or how outlandish your callings may seem, do you have enough faith to do it? Proverbs 3:5 (NKJV) tells us, "Trust in the Lord with all your heart, and lean not on your own understanding …" Though God's assignments for you may seem new or completely outside your comfort zone, you have to trust God so much that you will do whatever it takes to fulfill your purpose, even if that means doing something painful, out of the ordinary, or seemingly crazy.

And lastly, we have discovered that God expects each of us to pursue our mission with fervency, zeal, and a whole heart. God will not be satisfied if we only pursue some of our callings or if we only pursue them halfway—it is all or nothing, and God wants everything. I think the discussion of our calling can best be summarized by the words of the wise King Solomon. In Ecclesiastes 9:10, Solomon tells us, "Whatever your hand finds to do, do it with all your might."

You've heard God calling, and you know what He wants you to do. Will you do it? Will you put your desires, your preconceived notions, and your preferences aside for the sake of Christ? The people in the book of Acts did. The people in the book of Acts defied the "wisdom" of society, put aside their personal wants, and devoted every aspect of their lives to the service of Christ. And because of this, God used them to completely revolutionize the world we live in. God can use you to do the same, and it is my prayer that whatever He is calling you to do, you do with all your might because God's next revolution is only one calling away.

Printed in the United States
By Bookmasters